I. Introduction

This is the first in a series of reports by the Majority and Minority staff of the Senate Committee on Homeland Security and Governmental Affairs (Committee) on the threat of homegrown terrorism inspired by violent Islamist extremism. The Committee initiated an investigation into this threat during the 109th Congress under the leadership of Chairman Susan Collins (R-ME). The first hearing on the homegrown threat considered the potential for radicalization in U.S. prisons, including an examination of the activities of Kevin Lamar James, an American citizen. While in prison, James adopted a variant of violent Islamist ideology, founded an organization known as the Assembly for Authentic Islam (or JIS, the Arabic initials for the group), and began converting fellow prisoners to his cause. Upon release, James recruited members of JIS to commit at least 11 armed robberies, the proceeds from which were to be used to finance attacks against military installations and other targets in southern California. James and another member of the group eventually pled guilty to conspiring to wage war against the United States.

The James case is only one example of how the violent Islamist terrorist threat has evolved and expanded since the terrorist attacks of September 11, 2001. Al-Qaeda planned the 9/11 attacks and recruited the hijackers abroad before sending them to the United States to make final preparations for the operation. The 9/11 hijackers were indoctrinated into the violent Islamist mindset long before they set foot in the United States. As the James case and others illustrate, however, radicalization is no longer confined to training camps in Afghanistan or other locations far from our shores; it is also occurring right here in the United States.

During the 110th Congress, under the leadership of Chairman Joseph Lieberman (ID-CT), the Committee continued its investigation into the threat of domestic radicalization and homegrown terrorism inspired by violent Islamist ideology. The Committee has held five more hearings exploring a range of subjects, including an assessment of the homegrown threat in the United States, the European experience with domestic radicalization, the federal government's efforts to counter the homegrown terrorist threat, the role of local law enforcement in responding to the threat, and the Internet's role in the radicalization process.[1]

This staff report concerns the last of these subjects – how violent Islamist terrorist groups like al-Qaeda are using the Internet to enlist followers into the global violent Islamist terrorist movement and to increase support for the movement, ranging from ideological support, to fundraising, and ultimately to planning and executing terrorist attacks. In the second section of this report, we examine the increasing number of homegrown incidents and the judgments of the intelligence and law enforcement communities that there will likely be additional homegrown threats in the future. The third section explores the four-step radicalization process through which an individual can be enticed to adopt a violent Islamist extremist mindset and act on the ideology's call to violence. Section four identifies the disturbingly broad array of materials available on the Internet that promote the violent Islamist extremist ideology. The availability of these resources is not haphazard, but is part of a comprehensive, tightly controlled messaging campaign by al-Qaeda and like-minded extremists designed to spread their violent message. The fifth section of the report examines how these materials facilitate and encourage the radicalization process.

Finally, the report assesses the federal government's response to the spread of the violent Islamist message on the Internet and concludes that there is no cohesive and comprehensive outreach and communications strategy in place to confront this threat. The report does not discuss relevant classified tools and tactics employed by the law enforcement and intelligence communities, but does recognize that there is no plan to harness all possible resources including adopting new laws, encouraging and supporting law enforcement and the intelligence community at the local, state, and federal levels, and more aggressively implementing an outreach and counter-messaging campaign on the Internet and elsewhere.

II.   The Emerging Homegrown Terrorist Threat

Violent Islamist ideology and the terrorism it inspires pose a substantial threat to America's homeland security. The core tenets of this violent ideology are straightforward, uncompromising, and absolute. The ideology calls for the pursuit and creation of a global Islamist state – a Caliphate – that unites all Muslims – the *Ummah* – and is governed by Islamic law – *Sharia*. In pursuing this totalitarian goal, violent Islamists are not only encouraged to attack those who are not committed to their ideology in its purest form, including other Muslims, but are purportedly obligated to do so.[2]

Violent Islamist terrorists have attacked the United States and its interests many times. The first World Trade Center bombing in 1993, the attacks on the United States embassies in Kenya and Tanzania in 1998, the attack on the *USS Cole* in 2000, the devastating attacks of September 11, 2001, and many others were carried out by well-organized, well-equipped, and well-trained individuals indoctrinated into violent Islamist ideology. The United States government has appropriately focused its attentions at its borders and abroad, disrupting terrorist planning, training, and operations as part of the Global War on Terror. Despite these efforts, the Committee's investigation has found that the violent Islamist threat to the homeland has evolved and expanded.[3]

The attacks in Madrid, Spain, on March 11, 2004, and in London, England, on July 7, 2005, heralded a new form of the violent Islamist threat. In these attacks, homegrown terrorists – violent Islamist extremists living legally in the countries where the attacks took place – bombed public transportation facilities, killing their neighbors, and for some of the attackers, their fellow citizens. Homegrown terrorists inspired by this violent ideology also have planned and, in some cases, carried out attacks in other countries, including Germany, the Netherlands, France, Denmark, and Canada.

The United States has not been immune from homegrown threats, as evidenced by the James case and other incidents. For example:

- In December 2006, Derrick Shareef, a resident of Genoa, Illinois, who was not alleged to be part of a terrorist organization but was inspired by violent Islamist ideology, was charged with, and ultimately pleaded guilty to attempting to acquire explosives as part of a plan to attack the Cherry Vale Mall in Rockford, Illinois.
- In May 7, 2007, a group of six men were arrested as part of an alleged plot to attack the Fort Dix military base in New Jersey. The men – three of whom were legally living in the United States – allegedly watched violent Islamist videos, obtained weapons, and planned and trained for the attack in Pennsylvania and New Jersey.

- In June 2007, federal law enforcement disrupted an ideologically inspired terrorist plot to allegedly destroy fuel supplies and pipelines at John F. Kennedy International Airport in New York.

These incidents and others form part of a growing trend that has raised concerns within the U.S. intelligence and law enforcement communities. The Director of National Intelligence, Mike McConnell, and the Director of the Federal Bureau of Investigation, Robert S. Mueller, discussed this dangerous trend before the Senate Select Committee on Intelligence on February 5, 2008. Director McConnell testified that:

> Over the next year, attacks by "homegrown" extremists inspired by militant Islamic ideology but without operational direction from al-Qa'ida will remain a threat to the United States or against U.S. interests overseas. The spread of radical Salafi Internet sites that provide religious justification for attacks, increasingly aggressive and violent anti-Western rhetoric and actions by local groups, and the growing number of radical, self-generating cells in Western countries that identify with violent Salafi objectives, all suggest growth of a radical and violent segment among the West's Muslim populations.... The al-Qaida-propagated narrative of an "us versus them" struggle serves both as a platform and a potential catalyst for radicalization of Muslims alienated from the mainstream U.S. population.

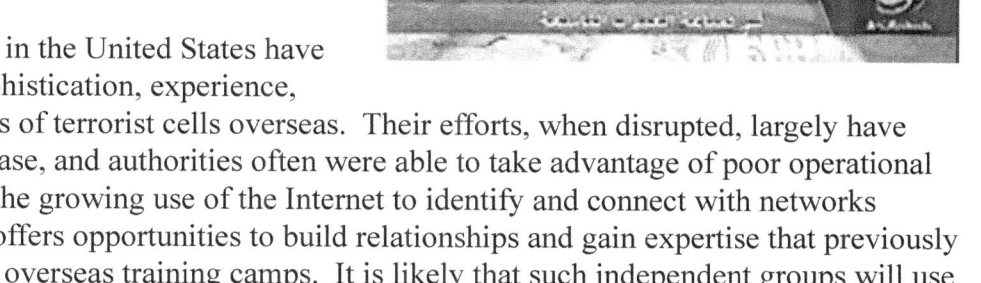

> ***

> To date, cells detected in the United States have lacked the level of sophistication, experience, and access to resources of terrorist cells overseas. Their efforts, when disrupted, largely have been in the nascent phase, and authorities often were able to take advantage of poor operational tradecraft. However, the growing use of the Internet to identify and connect with networks throughout the world offers opportunities to build relationships and gain expertise that previously were available only in overseas training camps. It is likely that such independent groups will use information on destructive tactics available on the Internet to boost their own capabilities.[4]

And, according to Director Mueller:

> [W]e face the challenges presented by a third group and that is self-radicalized, homegrown extremists in the United States. While not formally affiliated with a foreign terrorist group, they are inspired by those groups' messages of violence, often through the Internet, and because they lack formal ties, they are often particularly difficult to detect.[5]

III.   A Path to Radicalization

Homegrown terrorists are not created overnight. In order to fully identify the best way to combat this threat, the Committee sought to understand the process by which individuals or groups of individuals are radicalized to become violent Islamist extremists. The spark for the radicalization process is the core enlistment message that the leaders of the global violent Islamist terrorist movement use to attract followers. That terrorist message conveys the following three incendiary points:

- The West, led by the United States, is engaged in a war against Islam;

- Muslims are obligated to defend their religion and there are theological justifications for doing so; and

- Violence is the necessary means to defend the religion.[6]

After more than two years of research into homegrown terrorism cases in the United States and around the world, the New York City Police Department (NYPD) developed a model to explain how this core enlistment message, and the "jihadi-Salafi" ideology that provides the foundation for that message, drive the domestic radicalization process – transforming "unremarkable people" into terrorists.[7] During the Committee's October 30, 2007, hearing, the NYPD outlined this four-stage model:

> Pre-Radicalization: … [T]he point of origin for individuals before they begin the radicalization process. It is their life situation before they were exposed to and adopted jihadi-Salafi [ideology] … as their own ideology.

> Self-Identification: … [T]he phase where individuals, influenced by both internal and external factors, begin to explore Salafi Islam, gradually gravitate away from their old identity, and begin to associate themselves with like-minded individuals and adopt this ideology as their own.

> Indoctrination: … [T]he phase in which an individual progressively intensifies his beliefs, wholly adopts jihadi-Salafi ideology and concludes, without question, that the conditions and circumstances exist where action is required to support and further the cause… While the initial self-identification process may be an individual act, … association with like-minded people is an important factor as the process deepens.

> Jihadization: … [T]he phase in which members of the cluster accept their individual duty to participate in [terrorist activities] and self-designate themselves as holy warriors or mujahedeen. Ultimately, the group will begin operational planning for the … terrorist attack. These "acts in furtherance" will include planning, preparation and execution.[8]

According to testimony presented to the Committee, this process has been less likely to occur in the United States than in other countries. Some attribute this to the unique cultural influence of the "American experience" and the general absence of a sympathetic audience in the United States. For the most part, America's diverse Muslim communities are well integrated into our society and want to raise their families in safe and peaceful communities. And unlike some countries in Europe and elsewhere, the "longstanding tradition of absorbing varied diaspora populations has protected the United States and retarded the radicalization process at home."[9] Nonetheless, the recent rise in acts of homegrown terrorism planning and plotting in the United States may be an early warning that domestic radicalization inspired by violent Islamist ideology has become more likely in the United States. Assessments by both the law enforcement and intelligence communities support the conclusion that the United States will likely face increased levels of homegrown terrorist threats as violent Islamist extremists develop new methods to spark the radicalization process. Indeed, as the terrorists' Internet campaign bypasses America's physical borders and undermines cultural barriers that previously served as a bulwark against al-Qaeda's message of hate and violence, the threat of homegrown terrorist attacks in the United States increases.[10]

IV.   The Terrorist Internet Campaign

Propaganda has always been integral to the violent Islamist movement, especially for the purpose of attracting followers. Printed materials, videos of terrorist activities, including operations and training, and recordings of sermons and speeches espousing the virtues of the violent Islamist ideology have been distributed and sold around the world for decades.[11] But today, for an individual seeking information on this ideology, the Committee found that the Internet provides the most accessible source of information – both passive, in the form of static Web pages, and interactive, in the form of chat rooms and discussion forums that can connect interested individuals with extremists around the world.

The use of the Internet by violent Islamist extremists is constantly in flux, with websites appearing and disappearing regularly. Yet despite the dynamic nature of the websites, there is a generally organized framework for the dissemination of the core terrorist enlistment message. For those who want to know more about violent Islamist ideology, immense caches of information and propaganda are available online. Some material is produced by organized groups committed to advancing this ideology around the world, while other material is produced by self-starting individuals, who themselves may have "signed on" to the ideology's virtual network. These self-appointed amplifiers of the violent Islamist message may not be part of a known terrorist organization, but they choose to advance the cause, not necessarily with guns but with propaganda. Much of this material is readily available through web searches and is often discussed in chat rooms and other online forums where those interested in learning more about the violent Islamist ideology begin the radicalization process and seek out like-minded individuals.

A.   Al-Qaeda's Operation

Today, al-Qaeda manages a multi-tiered online media operation in which a number of production units associated with al-Qaeda or allied violent Islamist organizations produce content consistent with the core terrorist enlistment message. This sophisticated structure is a natural outgrowth of al-Qaeda's previous multimedia efforts. Al-Qaeda has long had a media committee[12] and once operated the now defunct www. alneda.com, which pushed the core terrorist enlistment message and disseminated official statements from al-Qaeda leadership.[13] Al-Qaeda also recognized, prior to 9/11, the value of videotaping attacks and disseminating the statements of terrorists who kill themselves in the name of violent Islamist ideology. Post 9/11, al-Qaeda leadership has accelerated their media campaign as

As-Sahab's Interview with Shakh Ayman Al-Zawahiri

necessary to pursuing their global ideological cause. In what is now a well-known letter to the former al-Qaeda commander in Iraq, Abu Musab al-Zarqawi, Ayman al-Zawahiri wrote, "We are in a battle, and more than half of this battle is taking place in the battlefield of the media. And that we are in a media battle in a race for the hearts and minds of our people."[14]

Several examples of al-Qaeda affiliated regional production centers include:

- Al-Furquan Media (affiliated with The Islamic State of Iraq)
- As-Sahab Media (affiliated with al-Qaeda High Command)
- Media Commission or Media Committee (affiliated with al-Qaeda in the Land of the Islamic Maghreb)
- Sawt al-Jihad (affiliated with al-Qaeda in the Arabian Peninsula)[15]

These production centers, which often include an icon or logo to identify themselves and their propaganda, are highly sophisticated operations that utilize cutting-edge technology. Videos may be relatively straightforward recordings of attacks, or they may be intricate productions with graphics, sound effects, banners, subtitles, animation, and stock footage. These centers also produce online magazines, official statements, news updates, articles, white papers, and even poetry. The use of songs, symbols, and imagery is integral, adding layers of meaning and emotion to what is being seen or heard.

Once content is created by as-Sahab, al-Furquan, or one of the other production units, it is then funneled through a clearinghouse before it is posted on the Internet. One of the most active Internet clearinghouses today is the al-Fajr Media Center, which was established in January 2006. Like the production centers, al-Fajr is almost entirely virtual. The approval process for dissemination is unclear, but once approved, content is moved from al-Fajr to pre-approved websites. On a daily basis, al-Fajr issues a host of material including statements from violent Islamist groups taking credit for attacks in Iraq, Afghanistan, Algeria, and elsewhere.[16]

These terrorist groups use clearinghouses for two primary reasons. First, along with the icons and logos that identify production centers, clearinghouses help ensure a message's authenticity.[17] A product released by al-Fajr is recognized as "genuine" and helps maintain message discipline. Because the violent Islamist movement is committed to its strict interpretation of the religion and its long-term goal to destroy the West, message discipline helps prevent deviation from either. Second, the clearinghouse process facilitates the near-instantaneous dissemination of new propaganda. Content approved by a clearinghouse is posted on pre-approved web forums like al-Ekhlaas, al-Hesbah, al-Buraq, or al-Firdaws that include some of the most "exclusive" violent Islamist websites – where access is tightly controlled.[18] The "approved" message is then reposted all over the Internet to become the subject of discussion and debate.[19]

The propaganda regularly produced by this process finds its way to literally *thousands* of violent Islamist websites across the Internet, many of which are either "mirrored" versions of one another or "simply bulletin boards" that disseminate the same material created by the production houses.[20] This distribution system provides built-in redundancies so that propaganda remains accessible even if one or more of the sites are not available.

Twin suicide bombings in Algeria on December 11, 2007, and a subsequent suicide bombing on January 29, 2008, illustrate how this propaganda dissemination process works. Al-Zawahiri announced in 2006 that the Salafist Group for Preaching and Fighting in Algeria had officially aligned with al-Qaeda.[21] In forming the alliance, the group assumed the new name al-Qaeda in the Land of the Islamic Maghreb and reinvigorated its online operation with the creation of the Media Commission. Very soon after the Algerian attacks, the Media Commission released statements through al-Fajr taking credit for the attacks and providing background and pictures of the suicide bombers. Al-Fajr posted the statement online where it was then viewed and disseminated around the world. The statements included quotes from the Koran, celebrated the attacks themselves, and hit all three points of the core terrorist enlistment message.

Al-Qaeda also uses its online campaign to bypass traditional media and speak "directly" to followers, in part because the terrorist groups believe their message is diluted when replayed or reported by news outlets.[22] In December 2007, al-Zawahiri announced in an as-Sahab produced video that he would answer questions submitted by followers via some of the more exclusive web forums. In a subsequent as-Sahab video released on April 2, 2008, al-Zawahiri tried to address certain issues that were undermining al-Qaeda's credibility among its supporters, including al-Qaeda's responsibility for killing innocent Muslims and the writings of Sayid Imam al-Sharif. In his new book, al-Sharif, a one-time proponent of violent Islamist ideology and a religious mentor to al-Zawahiri, renounced violence as ineffective and religiously unlawful for the purpose of forcing political change. Al-Zawahiri not only tried to discredit al-Sharif's new position in his video response, he also released a book on the Internet purporting to refute many of al-Sharif's arguments.[23]

Over the last year, al-Qaeda also made a tactical decision to increase its production of online propaganda and make more of it accessible to English-speaking audiences. Al-Qaeda has sought out English translators and, according to Charlie Allen, the Chief Intelligence Officer at the Department of Homeland Security (DHS), al-Qaeda has "ratcheted up the speed and accuracy of translated statements openly marketed to U.S. and English-speaking audiences."[24] For example, al-Qaeda has added subtitles to its video products and made appeals directly to Americans, including specific religious, ethnic, and racial populations in the United States and elsewhere. On September 8, 2007, as-Sahab released a video of an Osama bin Laden monologue titled "Message to the American People."

This video followed the as-Sahab release of an interview with al-Zawahiri, in which he made the following plea:

> That's why I want blacks in America, people of color, American Indians, Hispanics, and all the weak and oppressed in North and South America, in Africa and Asia, and all over the world, to know that when we wage Jihad in Allah's path, we aren't waging Jihad to lift oppression for the Muslims only, we are waging Jihad to lift oppression from all of mankind, because Allah has ordered us never to accept oppressions, whatever it may be.

According to Dr. Jarret Brachman, the Director of Research at the Combating Terrorism Center at West Point, one goal of this tactical decision was to attract particular groups al-Qaeda perceives as "self-starting radicals who [could] reach back to A[l] Q[aeda's] high-command, much like we saw in London with Operation Crevice and the 7/7 attacks."[25] DHS' Chief Intelligence Officer, Mr. Allen, also recognizes a similar intent in the changes to al-Qaeda's recent propaganda campaign, which has been assisted by supporters in the United States:

> Al-Qaeda's leadership has delivered over the past twelve months, an unprecedented number of audio and video messages and has increased its translation capability, diversity of subject matters, and media savvy to reach out to wider audiences globally. Its objective is to gain wide Muslim support, empathy, financing, and future recruits. … To help al-Qaeda target U.S. citizens, several radical websites in the United States have re-packaged al-Qaeda statements with American vernacular and commentary intending to sway U.S. Muslims.[26]

B.   The Purveyors of Violent Islamist Ideology

The Internet hosts a vast electronic repository of texts and treatises by the zealots who have given shape to the supposed theological justifications for violent Islamist ideology and the strategies for advancing its cause. These zealots and their ideas, which have inspired attacks in the West and elsewhere, are considered by some to be the "center of gravity" of the violent Islamist movement, more so perhaps than bin Laden or al-Zawahiri.[27] According to testimony received by the Committee, websites that host this material "allow the Internet to function as a kind of virtual extremist *madrassa*" enlisting and inspiring followers around the world.[28]

One such leader is Abu Muhammad al-Maqdisi, a formally trained cleric who served as the spiritual guide for al-Zarqawi, al-Qaeda's former commander in Iraq. Al-Maqdisi created, and his followers have maintained, a website dedicated to the cleric that includes a large library of downloadable books on the supposed theological justifications for violent Islamist ideology.[29] Links to English translations of al-Maqdisi's writings and many other violent Islamist zealots like Abu Qatada al-Filistini,[30] Abdullah Azzam, or Sayid Imam, have been made readily available online by at-Tibyan Publications, which appears to be a global distribution network of like-minded multilingual supporters of violent Islamist ideology who have taken it upon themselves to translate texts and make them available to Western audiences.[31] At-Tibyan Publications appears to have been at least one of the organizations to translate the English version of *39 Ways to Serve and Participate in Jihad*. This online text has been one of their most popular and widely disseminated publications.[32]

The at-Tibyan Publications website also has a list of "recommended scholars" that include al-Zarqawi, Sayid Qutb – whose writings help lay the foundation for contemporary violent Islamist ideology – and one of the leading but lesser known violent Islamist "scholars" named Abu Musab al-Suri. Al-Suri, a one-time associate of bin Laden who was connected to the March 11, 2004, bombings in Madrid, wrote a 1,600-page screed entitled *The Call for Global Islamic Resistance*. In addition to recapping the history of the violent Islamist movement, al-Suri's text, which has been heavily discussed online, prescribes ways to advance the cause of the ideology in a post 9/11 global environment. Al-Suri's propaganda includes the creation of global Islamic resistance brigades – isolated cells committed to advancing the violent Islamist extremist agenda.

Though many of the zealots whose writings have been made available by at-Tibyan Publications have been killed or captured, their ideas persist, and the Internet has played a role in keeping those ideas alive and proliferating them with increasing momentum. The organization of the Internet campaign has also helped retain message discipline outside of al-Qaeda's efforts. For example, at-Tibyan Publications did not release al-Sharif's most recent writings, which undermined the terrorists' use of violence, posting instead his earlier writings espousing violence as a necessary tactic for the global violent Islamist movement.

C.   Other Violent Islamist Media

Other material available online may be less doctrinal or structured. However, much of it appears designed to appeal to younger audiences who may be the most vulnerable to the influence of the core

terrorist enlistment message. One of the older and more prolific media organizations is the Global Islamic Media Front (GIMF). This group, which does not appear to have any official connections to al-Qaeda leadership, produces and distributes violent Islamist material designed to inform, inspire, and recruit followers into the global violent Islamist movement. GIMF tries to reach as wide an audience as possible by disseminating material in different languages and by tailoring its content to appeal to a range of nationalities, educational backgrounds, and age groups. Original content produced by GIMF may include religious, military, or ideological texts, online magazines, and videos of speeches

and military operations. At one point, the GIMF also broadcast a streaming television broadcast called the Caliphate Voice Channel. One of GIMF's most popular products was a videogame called "The Night of Bush Capturing," the object of which is to hunt and kill the President of the United States.[33]

Followers of the ideology also produce content that supports the goals of violent Islamists. One of the most well-known examples is the rap video "Dirty Kuffar" (Kuffar means "nonbeliever"), which was downloaded onto millions of computers or watched online.[34] In the video, the rapper, waving a gun and a Koran, praises bin Laden and the 9/11 attacks and disparages Western leaders with lyrics such as:

> Peace to Hamas and the Hezbollah
> OBL pulled me like a shiny star
> Like the way we destroyed them two towers ha-ha
> The minister Tony Blair, there my dirty Kuffar
> The one Mr. Bush, there my dirty Kuffar
> Throw them on the fire.[35]

The song is performed against a changing backdrop of images of world leaders morphing into animals or fictional characters and scenes of terrorists engaging in military training and attacking coalition forces in Iraq.

D.   Chat Rooms

With the proliferation of violent Islamist ideology on the Internet, anyone looking to learn more about the ideology can easily find it online. For those enticed by its message, either through the Internet or from another source, a likely first stop on the web would be one of the chat rooms or other online discussion forums that "are now supplementing and replacing mosques, community centers, and coffee shops as venues for recruitment and radicalization."[36] Access to chat rooms, however, is tightly controlled. Several layers of validation are often required before access may be granted.[37] Topics of discussion are also restricted, and dissenting views are rarely tolerated. Chat rooms also allow for potential followers to maintain their anonymity, which helps draw in a much wider audience. Though young males constitute a solid majority of those participating in these forums, women are becoming increasingly active.[38] Once individuals are admitted to them, chat rooms offer users access to each other and to the global violent Islamist virtual network.

V.   A Virtual Terrorist Training Camp

The violent Islamist Internet campaign facilitates the exposure of potential followers to the ideology. It allows leaders of the movement to talk directly to those who may be vulnerable to the influences of the core terrorist enlistment message without having the ideology filtered through intermediaries, like community leaders or media outlets.[39] And after that introduction, the Internet can play a critical role throughout the radicalization process, the potential end point of which is planning and executing a terrorist act.

In a July 2007 National Intelligence Estimate, entitled *The Terrorist Threat to the US Homeland,* the Intelligence Community assessed:

> [T]he spread of radical – especially Salafi – Internet sites, increasingly aggressive anti-US rhetoric and actions, and the growing number of radical, self-generating cells in Western countries indicate that the radical and violent segment of the West's Muslim population is expanding, including in the United States. The arrest and prosecution by US law enforcement of a small number of violent Islamic extremists inside the United States – who are becoming more connected ideologically, virtually, and/or in a physical sense to the global extremist movement – points to the possibility that others may become sufficiently radicalized that they will view the use of violence here as legitimate.[40]

In testimony before the U.S. House of Representatives, Dr. Thomas Fingar, the Deputy Director of National Intelligence for Analysis, further explained the potential link between a rise in homegrown terrorism and the Internet:

> [T]he growing use of the Internet to identify and connect with networks throughout the world offers opportunities to build relationships and gain expertise that previously were available only in overseas training camps. It is likely that such independent groups will use information on destructive tactics available on the Internet to boost their own capabilities.[41]

In presenting the NYPD report on violent Islamist extremism to the Committee, Lawrence Sanchez, the Assistant Commissioner of NYPD's Intelligence Division, testified that the Internet has become the most significant factor in the radicalization process in America today and can play a role in all four steps of that process.[42] According to the NYPD report:

> As individuals progress through the various [radicalization] stages, their use of the Internet evolves as well. In the Self-Identification phase, the Internet serves chiefly as the person's source of information about Islam and a venue to meet other seekers online. With the aggressive proliferation of the jihadi-Salafi ideology online, it is nearly impossible for someone to avoid this extreme interpretation of Islam.

> During the Indoctrination phase those undergoing this self-imposed brainwashing devote their time in the cyber world to the extremist sites and chat rooms – tapping into virtual networks of like-minded individuals around the world who reinforce the individual's beliefs and commitment
> and further legitimize them. At this stage, individuals or the groups they are in are likely to begin proliferating jihadi-Salafist ideology online along with consuming it. The Internet becomes a virtual "echo chamber" – acting as a radicalization accelerant while creating the path for the ultimate stage of Jihadization.

> In the Jihadization phase, people challenge and encourage each others' move to action. The Internet is now a tactical resource for obtaining instructions on constructing weapons, gathering information on potential targets, and providing spiritual justification for an attack.[43]

The Committee's own investigation identified ways in which the Internet campaign can play a significant – if varying – role in each of these four stages.

A.   Pre-Radicalization and Self-Identification

Pre-radicalization and self-identification involve an individual becoming exposed to and exploring violent Islamist ideology. Once individuals start exploring, the terrorists' coordinated online media campaign provides ready access to the core enlistment message, which is meant to appeal to those who may be asking questions about their background or heritage.[44] The violent Islamist extremist answer to these questions is stark – there is only friend or foe, a direct reflection of the violent Islamist ideology that seeks to purge the religion "of all outside influences, starting with the cultures and traditions of contemporary Muslim societies, and restore it to that of an imagined 7th Century utopia."[45] There is little, if any, room for debate; just the opportunity to learn more about why a call to violent action is supposedly consistent with religious principles. The militant component of the message also taps into youthful idealism by offering the possibility of glorious martyrdom in defense of the religion and the pursuit of the mythical perfect society.[46] With online propaganda that is often flashy, hi-tech, and interactive, the Internet has helped enable violent Islamists to deliver this message in a way that appeals to increasingly younger demographics.

B.   Indoctrination

Once individuals have begun the radicalization process, the Internet then provides opportunities for those who believe in the enlistment message to advance its cause. Followers of violent Islamist ideology have recognized that their movement will be more robust if they make it easier for more people to participate.[47] One of the most extraordinary examples of this occurred when "an Iraqi insurgent group held a website design contest among its worldwide supporters. The prize for the winner was to launch a rocket attack against a U.S. base in Iraq simply by clicking the mouse on their computer from the comfort of their own home."[48]

There is also the very popular and accessible online text *39 Ways to Serve and Participate in Jihad*, which, as noted earlier, is one of the most popular texts that was made available on the at-Tibyan Publications website. According to *39 Ways*, a supporter of violent Islamist ideology can aid the movement in myriad ways, including joining the movement in spirit, fundraising, or pursuing what *39 Ways* refers to as "electronic jihad." Electronic jihad not only entails participating in online chat rooms or disseminating propaganda, but it can also involve cyber attacks against enemy websites, a tactic that is creating a whole new breed of terrorist.[49]

39 Ways also encourages supporters to read and learn the teachings of violent Islamists like Abdullah Azzam, who was a spiritual mentor to bin Laden, and Abu-Qatada, who preached alongside Abu Hamza al-Masri at the now infamous Finsbury Park Mosque in London that counts Richard Reid and Zacarias Moussaoui as two of its former attendees. The text also encourages followers to engage in weapons training and to become physically fit – even laying out a suggested exercise regimen. Disturbingly, *39 Ways* also explains how followers of violent Islamist ideology can participate in the cause by "raising children to love jihad and those who wage it." This includes having children "[l]isten to tapes of sermons that discuss jihad-related topics such as martyrdom and the virtues of the martyr."[50]

C.   Jihadization

As noted in the NYPD report, the final stage of the radicalization process can eventually lead to operational planning for and participating in a terrorist attack. During this stage, the Internet can be a vital tool for communication, training, and propelling an individual toward violence.

The Internet also plays an increasingly critical role in linking radicalized individuals with the global Islamist terrorist movement – what Dr. Marc Sageman calls "[m]obilization through networks." According to Dr. Sageman:

> Over the past two or three years, face-to-face radicalization is being replaced by online radicalization. It is the interactivity of the group that changes people's beliefs, and such interaction is found in Islamist extremist forums on the Internet. The same support and validation that young people used to derive from their offline peer groups are now found in these forums which promote the image of terrorist heroes, link them to the virtual

social movement, give them guidance and instruct them in tactics. These forums, virtual market places for extremist ideas, have become the virtual "invisible hand" organizing terrorist activities worldwide. The true leader of this violent social movement is the collective discourse on a half dozen influential forums. They are transforming the terrorist movement, recruiting ever younger members and now more prominently women, who can participate in the discussions.[51]

Asked to expand on the role the Internet plays in the radicalization process, including whether the Internet increases the potential of radicalization in the United States, Dr. Sageman explained:

> The Internet plays a critical role in the radicalization of young Muslims into terrorists. This is a new phenomenon. The pre-9/11 al-Qaeda terrorists were radicalized through face to face interaction. After Iraq, and especially in the past three years, this interactive process of radicalization takes place online, in the jihadi forums. This online radicalization is certainly replacing face to face radicalization. The key to understanding this process is to realize that it is based on interactivity between the members, which makes the participants in the forums change their mind. Some of the participants get so worked up that they declare themselves ready to be terrorists. In a way, recruitment is self-recruitment, which is why we cannot stop it by trying to identify and arrest "recruiters." These self-recruited upstarts do not need any outsiders to try to join the terrorist social movement. Since this process takes place at home, often in the parental home, it facilitates the emergence of homegrown radicalization, worldwide.[52]

Once "plugged in" to these networks, followers of violent Islamist ideology can become radicalized and are better positioned to take steps toward a terrorist act.

The Internet played such a role for two Georgia Tech students in Atlanta who were able to move from their dorm rooms to online chat rooms where they were then able to self-enlist in the global violent Islamist movement. The students, both of whom were U.S. citizens, used the web to contact a group in Canada informally known as the "Toronto 18." The Toronto 18, who were originally identified because of their online activity, were alleged to have been planning multiple bombings and attacks against targets in Canada. The Georgia Tech students made contact on the web with members of the Toronto 18 and discussed possible attacks. The two students later traveled to Toronto to further these discussions and then to Washington, D.C., where they videotaped potential targets, including the World Bank headquarters, the Masonic Temple in Alexandria, Virginia, and an oil storage facility close to I-95. The surveillance footage of the targets was not only sent to the Toronto 18, but was also found on the computer of Younis Tsouli, a 23-year old of Moroccan descent residing in the United Kingdom. By the time of Tsouli's arrest in 2005, he had become a central player in the global violent Islamist online network and had gained the trust of, and directly assisted, al-Zarqawi in distributing videos of attacks in Iraq – all without ever having to leave his home.

The Internet also played a critical role in enlisting and radicalizing Derrick Shareef, who was charged with planning to acquire explosives to attack the Cherry Vale Mall in Rockford, Illinois. Shareef was radicalized in part through his relationship with Hassan Abu-Jihad, a former member of the U. S. Navy who was convicted on March 5, 2008, on federal charges of material support for terrorism and for disclosing classified information on naval ship movements. Abu-Jihad sent the classified information to the Azzam Publications website, which has been used to promote and fundraise for bin Laden, al-

Qaeda, and other terrorist organizations for nearly a decade. Abu-Jihad had also ordered videos from the website and watched the videos with Shareef while the two lived in Phoenix, Arizona. Abu-Jihad and Shareef also discussed acquiring weapons and planning attacks against military installations in the United States. The Internet provided Abu-Jihad with the portal through which he was able to participate in the global violent Islamist movement and recruit others like Shareef to its cause.

D.   Lone Wolves

Special note should also be made of the phenomenon of "lone wolves" and the Internet's influence on them. Even where radicalized individuals or groups of individuals do not actively communicate with other like-minded individuals around the world, the Internet can provide an invaluable "handbook" for lone wolf terrorists.[53] FBI Director Robert Mueller testified to the Committee that the Bureau is particularly concerned about such "lone wolf actor[s] ... not tied in with any particular group overseas."[54] The emergence of these self-generated violent Islamist extremists who are radicalized online presents a challenge for law enforcement because lone wolves are less likely to come to the attention of law enforcement. Combined with their lethal anonymity, these actors find a ready online guide to taking violent action, such as one post on a website that provided ten steps for how the "Lone Wolves of Al-Qaeda" could operate in America with the goal of mimicking the exploits of John Allen Muhammad, one of the Washington, D.C., snipers.[55]

These lone wolf actors are a particular challenge for local law enforcement – the organizations increasingly relied upon to help prevent homegrown terror attacks. First, most local law enforcement agencies do not have the resources and capabilities to know what is happening on the "virtual street corner."[56] Second, the increased opportunity to radicalize online without the knowledge of law enforcement is not just a threat to the community where the terrorist lives and plots, but to other communities that may be targeted.[57]

VI.   The U.S. Response

Homegrown terrorism in the United States has been hindered to some extent by certain cultural and community characteristics that have acted to discourage violent radicalization.[58] However, the sophisticated and organized Internet campaign being waged by violent Islamist extremists around the world has the potential to erode the effectiveness of those inherent national "defenses." By speaking directly to potential followers in the United States, al-Qaeda and others are able to control their message, suppress dissent, and offer a hateful worldview that dictates, based on a perversion of the Islamic faith, that violence is the only remedy to rectify perceived wrongs. Left unchallenged, it is very possible that the core terrorist enlistment message espoused over the Internet will drive more individuals in the United States all the way through the four stages of the radicalization process and encourage them to conduct actual terrorist attacks.

In June 2006, President Bush approved the National Implementation Plan (NIP), the goal of which was to unify and integrate government activities to address the terrorist threat, including the homegrown threat.[59] According to Admiral John Scott Redd, the former Director of the National Counterterrorism Center, "[t]he NIP serves as the nation's strategic blueprint for the war on terror and it integrates the full weight of our diplomatic, homeland security, law enforcement, financial and military activities, as well as intelligence."[60] As evident in Admiral Redd's description, the NIP recognizes that defeating terrorism, especially terrorism inspired by violent Islamist extremism, will require an array of government resources in addition to traditional classified counterterrorism tools and tactics used by the intelligence and law enforcement communities.[61]

Despite recognition in the NIP that a comprehensive response is needed, the U.S. government has not developed nor implemented a coordinated outreach and communications strategy to address the homegrown terrorist threat, especially as that threat is amplified by the use of the Internet.[62] According to testimony received by the Committee, no federal agency has been tasked with developing or implementing a domestic communications strategy.[63] While there are a series of outreach efforts being pursued by federal agencies, those efforts are limited, isolated, and not part of a strategic, government-wide policy to significantly minimize the influence of violent Islamist ideology in the United States. For example, the Office of Civil Rights and Civil Liberties (CRCL) at DHS meets regularly with religious and ethnic community leaders in approximately five major cities. At those meetings, CRCL listens to and tries to address the concerns of participants. Though the meetings are helpful in establishing relationships and promoting dialogue, they are self-initiated by CRCL and not part of a government-wide outreach effort to address the homegrown threat. In addition, CRCL's narrow mission and limited national presence prevent that program from serving as an effective government-wide force to counter the stark dictates of the terrorist ideology.

In addition, CRCL conducts the meetings more or less independently of the FBI, which already has substantial contact with communities throughout the country through its 56 field offices, each of which engages in outreach through the FBI's Community Relations Unit. Like the CRCL meetings, the FBI's outreach program is not specifically designed to prevent the violent Islamist ideology from inspiring homegrown attacks, nor should it be, according to Director Mueller.[64] Rather, the FBI program is designed to promote confidence in the government as a whole and, more specifically, the FBI.[65] Outside of CRCL's outreach efforts, DHS does communicate and occasionally work with other departments like the Department of State, the Department of the Treasury, and the Department of Justice, including the FBI, but those efforts are limited in scope. And finally, the efforts by CRCL and the FBI's Community Relations Unit are not tied into programs administered by local police departments, some of which are quite comprehensive.

VII.   Conclusion

As this report demonstrates, the use of the Internet by al-Qaeda and other violent Islamist extremist groups has expanded the terrorist threat to our homeland. No longer is the threat just from abroad, as was the case with the attacks of September 11, 2001; the threat is now increasingly from within, from homegrown terrorists who are inspired by violent Islamist ideology to plan and execute attacks where they live. One of the primary drivers of this new threat is the use of the Internet to enlist individuals or groups of individuals to join the cause without ever affiliating with a terrorist organization. As this homegrown terrorist threat evolves, so too must our response. Our nation's efforts must go beyond classified intelligence and law enforcement programs. Current efforts that rely on relatively uncoordinated outreach to American-Muslim communities and fragmented communications strategies must be improved. Indeed, the most credible voices in isolating and rejecting violent Islamist ideology are those of Muslim community leaders, religious leaders, and other non-governmental actors who must play a more visible and vocal role in discrediting and providing alternatives to violent Islamist ideology.

To defeat the new homegrown terrorist threat, the United States must carefully develop and implement the cohesive and comprehensive approach called for in the NIP and apply it to an effective outreach and communications strategy. We must isolate and discredit the violent Islamist ideology as a cause worth supporting, let alone a cause worth advancing by attacking and killing one's neighbors and fellow citizens. In developing such a strategy, the federal government must address several key questions including:

- What, if any, new laws, resources and tactics other than those already employed by intelligence and law enforcement should be used to prevent the spread of the ideology in the United States?

- What should a communications strategy, both on and off the Internet, look like, and what role, if any, should the government have in carrying out that strategy? What role must community and religious leaders play?

- What is the purpose of current outreach efforts, and how can those efforts improve, especially with increased coordination at all levels of government?

- What role should local officials and local law enforcement play given their longstanding relationships with the communities they serve and the fact that they are better positioned to recognize and intervene, if and when it is necessary to do so?

These are just a few of the pivotal questions that must be answered if the threat of homegrown terrorism inspired by violent Islamist ideology on the Internet is to be defeated. Over the past year, the law enforcement and intelligence communities have made it clear that they expect this threat to grow, especially as the Internet continues to be used to spread the terrorists' message, to enlist followers, and to provide more ways to pursue the terrorists' destructive goals. The United States must stay ahead of this threat by pursuing a national strategy to counter the influence of the ideology. This is a critical challenge for the homeland security of the United States; one the U.S. government must work quickly and aggressively to overcome. The safety of the American people depends on it.

[1] U.S. Senate, Committee on Homeland Security and Governmental Affairs, hearing on *The Threat of Islamic Radicalism to the Homeland*, Mar. 14, 2007; U.S. Senate, Committee on Homeland Security and Governmental Affairs, hearing on *The Internet: A Portal to Violent Islamist Extremism*, May 3, 2007; U.S. Senate, Committee on Homeland Security and Governmental Affairs, hearing on *Violent Islamist Extremism: Government Efforts to Defeat It*, May 10, 2007; U.S. Senate, Committee on Homeland Security and Governmental Affairs, hearing on *Violent Islamist Extremism: The European Experience*, June 27, 2007; U.S. Senate, Committee on Homeland Security and Governmental Affairs, hearing on *The Role of Local Law Enforcement in Countering Violent Islamist Extremism*, Oct. 30, 2007.

[2] Arvin Bhatt and Mitchell Silber, *Radicalization in the West: The Homegrown Threat*, New York City Police Department Intelligence Division, Aug. 15, 2007, p. 37 (submitted as a written statement for the Committee's hearing on *The Role of Local Law Enforcement in Countering Violent Islamist Extremism*, Oct. 30, 2007).

[3] According to Mr. Mitchell Silber, Senior Intelligence Analyst for the NYPD:

> The NYPD believes that the threat and the nature of the threat of al Qaeda-inspired terrorism to New York City has evolved since September 11, 2001. While the threat from overseas remains, most of the terrorist attacks or thwarted plots against cities in the West since 9/11 have fit a different pattern. The individuals who plotted or conducted the attacks were generally citizens or residents of the nations in which the attacks occurred. Though a few may have received training in al Qaeda camps, the great majority did not. Although al Qaeda claimed responsibility for each attack, these attacks were not under the command and control of al Qaeda central, nor were they specifically funded by al Qaeda central. Rather, they were conducted by local residents and citizens who used al Qaeda as their ideological inspiration. This is a homegrown threat, and it is driven by radicalization.

Testimony of Mr. Mitchell Silber, Senior Intelligence Analyst, NYPD, before the U.S. Senate, Committee on Homeland Security and Governmental Affairs, hearing on *The Role of Local Law Enforcement in Countering Violent Islamist Extremism*, Oct. 30, 2007. See also Written Statement of J. Michael McConnell, Director of National Intelligence, before the U.S. Senate, Select Committee on Intelligence, hearing on *Current and Projected National Security Threats*, Feb. 5, 2008, pp. 9-10; Testimony of Honorable Robert S. Mueller, III, Director, Federal Bureau of Investigation, before the U.S. Senate, Select Committee on Intelligence, hearing on *Current and Projected National Security Threats*, Feb. 5, 2008; National Intelligence Estimate, The Terrorist Threat to the Homeland, released July 2007; State of New Jersey Office of Homeland Security & Preparedness, *5th Annual Counter-Terrorism Conference –Radicalization: Global Trend...Local Concern?*, Oct. 12, 2007 (Key finding - "Radicalization exists in the United States and New Jersey and is a growing concern. There was a consensus among presenters and panelists that radicalization is present in the United States, including New Jersey, but none were prepared to quantify to what extent. Some pointed out that even one radicalized individual willing to do harm is significant. Most stated that they felt the problem was growing.").

[4] Written Statement of J. Michael McConnell, Director of National Intelligence, before the U.S. Senate, Select Committee on Intelligence, hearing on *Current and Projected National Security Threats*, Feb. 5, 2008, pp 9-10.

[5] Testimony of Honorable Robert S. Mueller, III, Director, Federal Bureau of Investigation, before the U.S. Senate, Select Committee on Intelligence, hearing on *Annual Worldwide Threat Assessment*, Feb. 5, 2008. See also prepared remarks of Robert S. Mueller, III, delivered at Chatham House, London, United Kingdom, Apr. 7. 2008, available at http://www.fbi.gov/pressrel/speeches/mueller040708.htm (last visited May, 5, 2008) ("The bottom tier is made up of homegrown extremists. They are self-radicalizing, self-financing, and self-executing. They meet up on the Internet instead of in foreign training camps. They have no formal affiliation with al Qaeda, but they are inspired by its message of violence. Examples of this tier include last year's plot to blow up pipelines at JFK airport in New York and a 2005 plot to attack military recruiting centers and a synagogue in Los Angeles.").

[6] Written Statement of Dr. Bruce Hoffman, Rand Corporation, before the U.S. House, Permanent Select Committee on Intelligence, hearing on *Terrorist Use of the Internet for Strategic Communications*, May 4, 2006, p. 6.

[7] The NYPD report defines "Salafi" as a "generic term, depicting a Sunni revivalist school of thought that takes the pious ancestors of the early period of early Islam as exemplary models. Consequently, Salafis seek to purge Islam of all outside influences, starting with the cultures and traditions of contemporary Muslim societies, and restore it to that of an imagined 7th Century utopia (the Caliphate). The Salafi interpretation of Islam seeks a 'pure' society that applies the Quran literally and adheres to the social practices and Islamic law (sharia) that prevailed at the time of the prophet Muhammad in the 7th century in Arabia." The report then defines "jihadi-Salafi" ideology as a "militant interpretation of the Salafi school of thought that

identifies violent jihad as the means to establish and revive the Caliphate. Militant jihad is seen not as an option, but as a personal obligation. This obligation is elevated above other moral standards, which may be abrogated." Supra note 2, pp. 5, 86.

[8] Supra note 2, pp. 6-7.

[9] Testimony of Mr. Mitchell Silber, Senior Intelligence Analyst, NYPD, before the U.S. Senate, Committee on Homeland Security and Governmental Affairs, hearing on *The Role of Local Law Enforcement in Countering Violent Islamist Extremism*, Oct. 30, 2007.

[10] Last year, the Pew Research Center released a report titled "Muslim Americans: Middle Class and Mostly Mainstream" that concludes in part that "Muslim Americans … are largely assimilated, happy with their lives, and moderate with respect to many of the issues that have divided Muslims and Westerners around the world. Muslim Americans are a highly diverse population, one largely compromised of immigrants. Nonetheless, they are decidedly American in their outlook, values and attitudes. Overwhelmingly, they believe that hard work pays off in this society. This belief is reflected in Muslim American income and education levels, which generally mirror those of the general public." However, the report also found that 27% of those polled refused to express an opinion of al-Qaeda while 5% actually had a favorable view of the terrorist organization. In addition, the report found that "8% of Muslim Americans say suicide bombings against civilian targets tactics are often (1%) or sometimes (7%) justified in the defense of Islam. Muslims in France, Spain and Great Britain were twice as likely as Muslims in the U.S. to say suicide bombing can be often or sometimes justified, and acceptance of the tactic is far more widespread among Muslims in Nigeria, Jordan and Egypt." Pew Research Center, *Muslim Americans: Middle Class and Mostly Mainstream*, released May 2007.

[11] Thomas Hegghammer, Research Fellow, Norwegian Defence Research Establishment, e-mail to Todd M. Stein, Counsel, Senate Committee on Homeland Security and Governmental Affairs, Dec. 21, 2007 (on file with Committee Staff).

[12] Al-Qaeda's media committee was once led by Khalid Sheikh Muhammad. According to the 9/11 Commission Report, "No one exemplifies the model of the terrorist entrepreneur more clearly than Khalid Sheikh Mohammad, the principal architect of the 9/11 attacks. KSM followed a rather tortuous path to his eventual membership in al-Qaeda. Highly educated and equally comfortable in a government office or a terrorist safehouse, KSM applied his imagination, technical aptitude, and managerial skills to hatching and planning an extraordinary array of terrorist schemes. These ideas included conventional car bombing, political assassination, aircraft bombing, hijacking, reservoir poisoning, and ultimately, the use of aircraft as missiles guided by suicide operators." National Commission on Terrorist Attacks upon the United States, *The 9/11 Commission Report*, p. 145, released July 22, 2004.

[13] Supra note 6.

[14] Craig Whitlock, "Keeping Al-Qaeda in His Grip," *Washington Post*, Apr. 16, 2006.

[15] Response to Committee Staff Questions, Dr. Jarrett Brachman, Director of Research, Combating Terrorism Center at West Point, Nov. 28, 2007 (on file with Committee Staff). See also Radio Free Europe/Radio Liberty, *The Al-Qaeda Media Nexus: The Virtual Network Behind the Global Message*, released Mar. 2008.

[16] Response to Committee Staff Questions, Dr. Jarrett Brachman, Director of Research, Combating Terrorism Center at West Point, Nov. 28, 2007 (on file with Committee Staff); Written Statement of Dir. Rita Katz, SITE Institute, before the U.S. House, Subcommittee on Intelligence, Information Sharing and Terrorism Risk Assessment, hearing on *Using the Web as a Weapon: the Internet as a Tool for Violent Radicalization and Homegrown Terrorism,* Nov. 6, 2007, pp. 6-8.

[17] Response to Committee Staff Questions, Dr. Jarrett Brachman, Director of Research, Combating Terrorism Center at West Point, Nov. 28, 2007 (on file with Committee Staff).

[18] *Id.*

[19] Testimony of Dr. Michael S. Doran, Deputy Assistant Secretary of Defense for Support for Public Diplomacy, U.S. Department of Defense, before the U.S. Senate, Committee on Homeland Security and Governmental Affairs, hearing on *The Internet: A Portal to Violent Islamist Extremism,* May 3, 2007; Response to Committee Staff Questions, Dr. Jarrett Brachman,

Director of Research, Combating Terrorism Center at West Point, Nov. 28, 2007 (on file with Committee Staff).

[20] Written Statement of Dr. Michael S. Doran, Deputy Assistant Secretary of Defense for Support for Public Diplomacy, U.S. Department of Defense, before the U.S. Senate, Committee on Homeland Security and Governmental Affairs, hearing on *The Internet: A Portal to Violent Islamist Extremism,* May 3, 2007, p. 1.

[21] Testimony of Judge Jean-Louis Bruguière, First Vice President, Investigating Magistrate, France, before the U.S. Senate, Committee on Homeland Security and Governmental Affairs, hearing on *Violent Islamist Extremism: The European Experience,* June 27, 2007.

[22] Supra note 6; see also Radio Free Europe/Radio Liberty, *The Al-Qaeda Media Nexus: The Virtual Network Behind the Global Message,* released Mar. 2008.

[23] Combating Terrorism Center at West Point, *The Power of Truth? Questions for Ayman al-Zawahiri,* Apr. 2008.

[24] Charles E. Allen, Chief Intelligence Officer and Under Secretary for Intelligence and Analysis, Department of Homeland Security, address to the Washington Institute for Near East Policy, "Terrorism in the Twenty-first Century: Implications for Homeland Security," May 6, 2008.

[25] Supra note 17.

[26] Supra note 24.

[27] Written Statement of Dir. Lt-Col Joseph H. Felter, Combating Terrorism Center, U.S. Military Academy, before the U.S. Senate, Committee on Homeland Security and Governmental Affairs, hearing on *The Internet: A Portal to Violent Islamist Extremism,* May 3, 2007, p. 4.

[28] Supra note 20, p. 3.

[29] Id.

[30] According to Dr. Marc Sageman, "Video cassettes of popular Salafi preachers, like Omar Mahmoud Oatham (a.k.a. abu Qatada), have been commonly found in apartments of arrested mujahedin." Marc Sageman, *Understanding Terror Networks,* University of Pennsylvania Press (2004), p. 160.

[31] The website for at-Tibyan Productions is http://tibyan.wordpress.com (last visited on May 5, 2008).

[32] Dr. Jarret Brachman, Director of Research, Combating Terrorism Center at West Point, e-mail to Todd M. Stein, Counsel, Senate Committee on Homeland Security and Governmental Affairs, Dec. 5, 2007 (on file with Committee Staff).

[33] Staff with the Norwegian Defence Research Establishment provided the Committee with the following background information on the GIMF:

> The Global Islamic Media Front (GIMF) was established in August 2004. It first operated from a website located in France, but the group has since relied on numerous IP addresses/websites. In recent years (2006-2007), GIMF has not had one official website, but rather operated on many affiliated sites, especially the jihadist web forums. The most recent GIMF-affiliated sties include blogs in Arabic, English, and German, as well as a German language forum. The declared goal of GIMF is to 'denounce the Zionist enemy' and to 'break the Zionist control over the media and terrorize the enemies.' … Recent arrests have revealed the identity (Austrian, Canadian) of some individuals reportedly linked to the GIMF. The identity of other members of the GIMF, working on the production of the group's media material, is unknown. … On several occasions, GIMF has allegedly posted job advertisements asking supporters to fill "vacant positions for video production and editing statements, footage and international media coverage about militants in Iraq, the Palestinian territories, Chechnya and other conflict zones where militants are active." The work of GIMF is thus most likely assisted by ordinary, technology-savvy supporters of the jihadist movement. It appears as a quite loosely organized network, which allows a large number of voices to be spread on the web. Jihadists who publish in the name of GIMF range from well-known jihadist sheikhs to

jihadist new-comers. There seems to be no official connection between GIMF and al-Qaeda leadership despite assessments by Western media that GIMF is an "al-Qaeda mouthpiece." GIMF regularly praises the al-Qaeda leadership, but does not publish statements or other issuances directly from "al-Qaeda Central". … GIMF publishes material that includes statements and video footage of operations of various jihadist groups. Lately, a majority of these groups have been Iraqi based insurgent groups, but also Somali jihadst groups and jihadists in Chechnya have been represented by GIMF. As far as we know, GIMF does not belong to, or officially cooperate with, any of these insurgent groups.

GIMF acts both as a producer and distributor of jihadist media material. As a distributor, the GIMF often redesigns and translates/subtitles productions, before spreading them on the jihadist web. … GIMF ensures wide online diffusion of material produced by other jihadist groups, generally, as mentioned above, after re-designing, translating, or subtitling the production. This indicates its vision of reaching the broadest possible public, including foreign language speakers. … As a producer of jihadist media, GIMF also seeks to reach a wide audience, albeit, first and foremost Arabic speakers. Yet GIMF differentiates between audiences of different educational levels and targets various age groups through its different productions and methods of persuasion. The main target group is still supporters and potential supporters of the jihadist movement. While GIMF productions are first and foremost distributed online, GIMF also encourages the distribution of printed material, as well as oral dissemination. As for the online media, GIMF is the jihadist media group that employs perhaps the widest range of means of communications: written texts, videos, TV broadcasts, and video games distributed to static websites, blogs and discussions forums, bear witness to a certain creativity.

Thomas Hegghammer, Research Fellow, Norwegian Defence Research Establishment, e-mail to Todd M. Stein, Counsel, Senate Committee on Homeland Security and Governmental Affairs, Dec. 21, 2007 (on file with Committee Staff).

[34] Omar El Akkad, "Terror Goes Digital," *Globe and Mail*, Aug. 18, 2007.

[35] The video of Dirty Kuffar is accessible http://www.youtube.com/watch?v=qKgkF7HkzNI (last visited on May. 5, 2008).

[36] Written Statement of Frank J. Cilluffo, Director, Homeland Security Police Institute, The George Washington University, before the U.S. Senate, Committee on Homeland Security and Governmental Affairs, hearing on *The Internet: A Portal to Violent Islamist Extremism*, May 3, 2007, p. 1.

[37] Supra note 20, p. 1.

[38] Written Statement of Dr. Marc Sageman, Principal, Sageman Consulting, LLC, before the U.S Senate, Committee on Homeland Security and Governmental Affairs, hearing on *Violent Islamist Extremism: The European Experience*, June 27, 2007, p. 4.

[39] Supra note 20, pp. 2-4.

[40] National Intelligence Estimate, *The Terrorist Threat to the Homeland*, July 2007.

[41] Written Statement of Dr. Thomas Fingar, the Deputy Director of National Intelligence for Analysis, before the U.S. House of Representatives, Committee on Armed Services, hearing on *Global Security Assessment*, Feb 13, 2008, pp. 9-10.

[42] In addition to identifying the Internet as the "most significant factor in the radicalization that is occurring in America," Assistant Commissioner Sanchez added:

I believe the Internet is usually the stepping stone where people go to look first. If you look across these phases of radicalization, there is an identity phase where people are really looking for an answer. When you look for an answer, people nowadays, especially in Western societies, go to the Internet. … Then the Internet plays another role. When you move to another state, which is one of looking for other like-minded people you can come out of the virtual world and meet real people, it has chat rooms. It talks about places. It talks about thing you could do together. It talks about events that you can go and join and become part of it. So now it gives you indicators for the real world where you can meet real people rather than living in this virtual world. And then as you progress down these stages, the Internet then becomes a research tool for maybe things you want to do. If you want to research information on bomb-making material, the Internet, again, becomes a resource for that. So it really covers the breadth of a radicalization process and becomes a useful tool in each of its phases.

Testimony of Lawrence Sanchez, Assistant Commissioner, Intelligence Division, NYPD, before the U.S. Senate, Committee on Homeland Security and Governmental Affairs, hearing on *The Role of Local Law Enforcement in Countering Violent Islamist Extremism*, Oct. 30, 2007.

[43] Supra note 2, p. 37.

[44] Testimony of Mr. Mitchell Silber, Senior Intelligence Analyst, New York City Police Department, before the U.S. Senate, Committee on Homeland Security and Governmental Affairs, hearing on *The Role of Local Law Enforcement in Countering Violent Islamist Extremism*, Oct. 30, 2007.

[45] Supra note 2, p. 86.

[46] Testimony of Dr. Marc Sageman, Principal, Sageman Consulting, LLC, before the U.S. Senate, Committee on Homeland Security and Governmental Affairs, hearing on *Violent Islamist Extremism:The European Experience*, June 27, 2007. Violent Islamist extremists often use the wars in Iraq and Afghanistan to enlist followers, but as Mitchell Silber, a senior intelligence analyst with the NYPD, explained in testimony to the Committee, the two wars are just the latest in a series of grievances violent Islamist extremists use to advance their cause:

> The list of grievances is long, and it includes issues like Spanish participation in Iraq, U.S. actions in Afghanistan and Iraq, Canadian or Australian participation in Afghanistan, U.S. support for Israel, British presence in Iraq or Afghanistan, and India's presence in Kashmir. However, it is important to note that the removal of any one or two of these issues would not eliminate the threat, and I call attention to the Madrid 2004 train bombings. Clearly, the number one grievance that drove these individuals was to punish Spain for its participation in the coalition war in Iraq. However, the second rationale is not as well known. The individuals who conducted the attack cited the Spanish occupation, and this is the Spanish occupation of al-Andalus going back to 1492 and the expulsion of the Moors by King Ferdinand and Queen Isabella – clearly a grievance that is unlikely to be resolved anytime soon.

Testimony of Mitchell Silber, Senior Intelligence Analyst, New York City Police Department, before the U.S. Senate, Committee on Homeland Security and Governmental Affairs, hearing on The *Role of Law Enforcement in Countering Islamic Extremism*, Oct. 30, 2007.

[47] Supra note 27, p. 5.

[48] Supra note 27, pp.5-6.

[49] *39 Ways to Serve and Participate in Jihad* is available in English at http://tibyan.wordpress.com/2007/08/24/39-ways-to-serve-and-participate-in-jihad/ (last visited May 5, 2008).

[50] Id.

[51] Supra note 38, p. 4.

[52] Questions for the Record of Dr. Marc Sageman, Principal, Sageman Consulting, LLC, before the U.S Senate, Committee on Homeland Security and Governmental Affairs, hearing on *Violent Islamist Extremism: The European Experience*, June 27, 2007, pp. 1-2.

[53] According to Dr. Sageman, there are incidences where followers of violent Islamist ideology have become radicalized solely through the Internet. Dr. Marc Sageman, Principal, Sageman Consulting, e-mail to Eric Andersen, Professional Staff Member, Senate Committee on Homeland Security and Governmental Affairs, Dec. 18, 1007 (on file with Committee Staff).

[54] Testimony of Honorable Robert S. Mueller III, Director, Federal Bureau of Investigation, U.S. Department of Justice, before the U.S. Senate, Committee on Homeland Security and Governmental Affairs, hearing on *Confronting the Terrorist Threat to the Homeland: Six Years After 9/11*, Sept. 10, 2007.

[55] The Middle East Media Research Institute, "The 'Lone Wolf' Theory and John Allen Muhammad," Nov. 21, 2007, available at http://www.memri.org/bin/articles.cgi?Page=subjects&Area=jihad&ID=SP177207 (last visited May 5, 2008).

[56] Testimony of Major Mike Ronczkowski, Homeland Security Bureau, Miami-Dade Police Department, before the U.S. Senate, Committee on Homeland Security and Governmental Affairs, hearing on *The Role of Local Law Enforcement in Countering Violent Islamist Extremism*, Oct. 30, 2007 ("[T]he Internet is a huge, huge dilemma for us. We cannot police [the Internet] at the local level."); Testimony of Deputy Chief Michael Downing, Counter Terrorism and Criminal Intelligence Bureau, Los Angeles Police Department, before the U.S. Senate, Committee on Homeland Security and Governmental Affairs, hearing on *The Role of Local Law Enforcement in Countering Violent Islamist Extremism,* Oct. 30, 2007 ("The LAPD must also have the capability to hunt for signs of radicalization and terrorism activities on the Internet, and we have recently started a cyber investigations unit to do just that. The Internet is the virtual hangout for radicals and terrorists.").

[57] Testimony of Lawrence Sanchez, Assistant Commissioner, Intelligence Division, New York City Police Department, before the U.S. Senate, Committee on Homeland Security and Governmental Affairs, hearing on *The Role of Local Law Enforcement in Countering Violent Islamist Extremism*, Oct. 30, 2007 ("We are hoping we have a handle on things that are incubating in the streets of Queens. But what we do not have confidence in is things that are incubating in the United States in another city who is not doing [what NYPD is doing] and who come to New York City as a target city.")

[58] Supra note 38, pp. 2-4.

[59] Michael E. Leiter, the Principal Deputy Director of the National Counterterrorism Center provided more detail about the National Implementation Plan in Congressional testimony:

> Our intent is to take the high-level strategic policy promulgated by the White House and translate that into coordinated, actionable tasks for departments and agencies to pursue their own mission. The principal, overarching result of this planning is, as the chairwoman has stated, a National Implementation Plan, or NIP, which was approved by the president in June of 2006. And I'm going to very briefly describe some of the key elements of the NIP. Let me first note that there are four parts to the NIP.
>
> And the first element is attacking terrorist capability overseas, the second is countering violent Islamic extremism, the third is protecting and defending the homeland, and the fourth is avoiding terrorist acquisition of WMD. Supporting all of these is what we call a cross-cutting enabler, and that is in fact promulgating and supporting our foreign partners in a way that our foreign partners can then in turn support our efforts overseas.
>
> Second, each of these four components is supported by very, very specific tasks, and each of those tasks is given, then, to a department or agency that has the responsibility for coordinating the interagency efforts. As we can talk about later, many of those actions that involve overseas work, involving law enforcement agencies and others are of course coordinated by the Department of State, which plays that role as a matter of statute.
>
> Third, we not only plan, but we do in fact seek to coordinate and integrate the synchronization of all these joint departmental activities.
>
> Fourth, the NIP is a planning document that is also used by the Office of Management and Budget, and OMB, in conjunction with NCTC, works with the NIP to make sure that department and agency programs are in fact supporting the tasks and objectives of the NIP.
>
> And finally, I want to stress one thing that the NIP and NCTC does not do, and this is a matter of statutory direction. We do not direct operational activity. We are in fact responsible for strategic operational planning, but ultimately, we rely on individual departments and agencies and their statutory authorities to carry out operations.

Testimony of Michael E. Leiter, Principal Deputy Director, National Counterterrorism Center, before the U.S. House of Representatives, Subcommittee on Border, Maritime and Global Counterrterrorism of the House Committee on Homeland Security, hearing on *Homeland Security Beyond Our Borders: Examining the Status of Counterrorism Coordination Overseas*, Oct. 4, 2007.

[60] Testimony of John Scott Redd, Director, National Counterterrorism Center, Office of the Director of National Intelligence, before the U.S. Senate, Committee on Homeland Security and Governmental Affairs, hearing on *Confronting the Terrorist Threat to the Homeland: Six Years After 9/11*, Sept. 10, 2007.

[61] Karen DeYoung, "A Fight Against Terrorism – and Disorganization," *The Washington Post*, July 9, 2006.

[62] The State Department's Counterterrorism Communications Center released a paper in March suggesting terminology for officials to use when talking about al-Qaeda inspired terrorism. DHS, once again through CRCL, drafted a similar paper in January. These documents were written independently of one another without the endorsement or affirmative input of the National Counterterrorism Center or the White House. In fact, President Bush, in subsequent remarks contradicted the premise of both papers, demonstrating that there is no government-wide strategic communications policy in place today. See also Testimony of Honorable John Scott Redd, Director, National Counterterrorism Center, Office of the Director of National Intelligence, before the U.S. Senate, Committee on Homeland Security and Governmental Affairs, hearing on *Confronting the Terrorist Threat to the Homeland: Six Years After 9/11*, Sept. 10, 2007.

[63] Supra note 60.

[64] Testimony of Honorable Robert S. Mueller III, Director, Federal Bureau of Investigation, U.S. Department of Justice, before the U.S. Senate, Committee on Homeland Security and Governmental Affairs, hearing on *Confronting the Terrorist Threat to the Homeland: Six Years After 9/11*, Sept. 10, 2007.

[65] Testimony of John Miller, Assistant Director, Office of Public Affairs, Federal Bureau of Investigation, U.S. Department of Justice, before the U.S. Senate, Committee on Homeland Security and Governmental Affairs, hearing on *Violent Islamist Extremism: Government Efforts to Defeat It*, May 10, 2007.

www.ingramcontent.com/pod-product-compliance
Lightning Source LLC
Chambersburg PA
CBHW080404290526
45790CB00009BA/3703